Using Exist

Read *Using Existing Ligh* and learn how to:

- Recognize the many varieties of existing light.

- Set your camera controls to get sharp, vivid photos in dimly lighted scenes.

- Take pictures in situations where flash would be distracting.

- Achieve natural-looking compositions.

THE NO NONSENSE LIBRARY

OTHER NO NONSENSE PHOTOGRAPHY GUIDES

Composing Photographs
Photographing People
Photographing Your Vacation
Using Accessory Equipment
Using Creative Techniques

OTHER NO NONSENSE GUIDES

Car Guides
Career Guides
Cooking Guides
Financial Guides
Health Guides
Legal Guides
Parenting Guides
Real Estate Guides
Study Guides
Success Guides
Wine Guides

NO NONSENSE PHOTOGRAPHY GUIDE™

USING EXISTING LIGHT

A KODAK Book

CAROLINE GRIMES

Longmeadow Press.

USING EXISTING LIGHT

Published by Longmeadow Press, 201 High Ridge Road, Stamford, Connecticut 06904. No part of this book may be reproduced or used in any form or by any means, electronic or mechanical, including photocopying, recording, or by an information storage and retrieval system, without permission in writing from the publisher.

No Nonsense Photography Guide is a trademark controlled by Longmeadow Press.

ISBN 0-681-40731-X

Copyright © 1990 by Eastman Kodak Company
All photographs © 1990 The Image Bank®.

Produced by The Image Bank in association with
Eastman Kodak Company, Rochester, New York.

Kodak is a registered trademark of
Eastman Kodak Company and is used under license from Kodak.

The Image Bank® is a registered trademark of The Image Bank, Inc.

Printed in Spain

0 9 8 7 6 5 4 3 2 1

Producer: Solomon M. Skolnick; *Editors:* Terri Hardin (The Image Bank), Margaret Buckley (Kodak), Derek Doeffinger (Kodak); *Production Director:* Charles W. Styles (Kodak); *Production Coordinator:* Ann-Louise Lipman (The Image Bank); *Editorial Assistant:* Carol Raguso; *Production Assistant:* Valerie Zars; *Photo Researcher:* Natalie Goldstein; *Copy Editor:* Irene S. Korn; *Art Direction and Design:* Chase/Temkin & Associates, Inc.

Cover photographs, left to right: Pamela J. Zilly, Jean-Pierre Pieuchot, George Obremski

For information about the photographs in this book, please contact:

The Image Bank
111 Fifth Avenue
New York, N.Y. 10003

Stockphotos, Inc.
373 Park Avenue South
New York, N.Y. 10016

TABLE OF CONTENTS

Introduction   6
**Part One: Preparing for Existing-Light
  Photography**   8
  Proper Exposure   11
  Time Exposures   18
  Choosing the Right Film   23
  Push-Processing   33
  Techniques for Getting Sharp Pictures   35
  Depth of Field   37
Part Two: Taking Pictures Indoors   38
  Home Lighting   40
  Light in Public Places   45
Part Three: Taking Pictures Outdoors   60
  Outdoor Scenes at Night   62
Glossary of Terms   78
Index   80

INTRODUCTION

Erik Leigh Simmons

How many times have you come upon a dimly lighted scene you knew would make a great photograph, but felt you lacked the proper equipment and knowledge?

In just a few brief pages, making images in such situations will no longer daunt you.

Strictly speaking, existing light covers all natural lighting—from moonlight to bright sunshine. But for photographic purposes, existing light means lighting situations characterized by lower light levels that require considerably more exposure than for subjects in most outdoor daylight conditions.

Existing light, sometimes called available light, generally means dim lighting. It includes artificial light that naturally exists in the scene, daylight indoors, and twilight outdoors. Any light that happens to be on the scene—from table and floor lamps, ceiling fixtures, and fluorescent lamps, to spotlights, candles, and fireplaces—is considered existing light, as well as outdoor scenes at twilight or after dark.

The advantages of existing-light photography are realism, versatility, and convenience. Existing-light pictures look realistic because you haven't altered the illumination in the scene. You can take pictures that aren't possible with other lighting techniques, such as flash. Subjects too far away for flash can be easily photographed by existing light because camera-to-subject distance won't affect your exposure as it would with a flash unit.

Existing-light picture-taking is inexpensive and convenient. Without lighting accessories, you can concentrate on your subjects, and you have greater freedom of movement.

Using Existing Light will help you explore situations where using flash would inhibit the people in your scene; and in situations where using existing light is the only way to photograph subjects beyond the range of flash.

Read through carefully and examine the photographic examples. Photographic terms with which you might be unfamiliar can be found in italics throughout the book and are listed in the glossary. This book will guide you toward a better understanding of the relationship of light to photography.

_____7

PART ONE

PREPARING FOR EXISTING-LIGHT PHOTOGRAPHY

Brett Froomer

Light, though important to all photography, is particularly crucial to existing-light situations. Therefore, the instruments by which light is measured and recorded are critical to getting the best images possible. Such instruments may include various hand-held meters, like the spot meter. The instrument of first importance, however, is the camera.

A 35 mm single-lens-reflex (SLR) camera is best suited for taking pictures in dim light. It can effectively use fast films; it lets you compensate for metering problems; and it lets you set the best combination of shutter speed and aperture to stop action or create front-to-back sharpness. Because most non-SLR cameras lack these capabilities, they are usually unsuitable for taking pictures in dim light. SLR cameras also usually have settings for long shutter speeds (or a "B" setting) for when you want to photograph fireworks, lightning, traffic patterns, or other light sources that have the capability of giving unusual effects with time exposures.

The second-most important piece of equipment to have—after the SLR camera—is the proper lens. While the appropriate lens depends on the type of photographs you intend to take, there are certain lenses that will serve as "catch-alls" within a wide variety of situations.

The normal (50 mm) lens, which is standard to the SLR camera, is also the best lens for existing-light photography. Its fairly large maximum aperture (typically about $f/1.8$) will gather lots of light not only making it possible to use a fast or moderate shutter speed, but also to see a relatively bright image in the viewfinder.

The advantage of a very large maximum aperture is that it gathers more light—a useful feature for photographing birthday cakes, sleeping babies, or other dim scenes. The disadvantages of a lens with a very large maximum aperture are its cost and weight.

With film speeds now topping ISO 1000, fast lenses (ones with a maximum aperture of $f/1.4$ or $f/1.2$) aren't quite as important as they used to be. That's good for two reasons: one, you

PREPARING FOR EXISTING LIGHT

A large maximum aperture will often admit enough light even in very dimly lighted situations.

don't have to pay extra money to get a fast lens; two, you can use a greater variety of lenses with these films, including many zoom lenses.

The drawbacks of less light provided by small maximum apertures are that you may be forced to use a tripod—and perhaps a cable release—because of a slow shutter speed; and you'll find it more difficult to see, and therefore compose, the dim image in the viewfinder.

With KODACOLOR GOLD 1600 Film, you may even be able to use a zoom lens with $f/5.6$ as its maximum aperture. But for versatility, try to use a lens with a maximum aperture of $f/2.8$ or larger.

In Part One, we will show you how to choose the right equipment and films for existing-light photography, as well as discuss the importance of the light source and finding the proper exposure for the mood you want to create.

USING EXISTING LIGHT

PROPER EXPOSURE

Reproducing existing-light scenes realistically can sometimes be a problem, especially with slide films since they have to be exposed precisely to accurately reproduce a scene. SLR cameras made in the last decade have built-in meters, and many of these cameras set exposure automatically. Since you'll often be overriding the exposure that the camera wants to set, review your camera manual to be sure you know how your camera meter measures light in a scene and how you can adjust the exposure.

Most camera meters are designed to give good exposures of uniformly brightly lit scenes. Existing-light scenes, however, tend to be either uniformly dim or a mixture of bright lights and very dark shadows. Getting proper exposures of such scenes often requires you to adjust the settings indicated by the meter.

Uniformly dim scenes. With uniformly dim scenes, the camera meter will probably indicate an exposure that lets too much light reach the film. If you have slide film in the camera, reduce the exposure by 1/2 to 1 stop so the slides will look as

Sean Smith/Stockphotos, Inc.

Since pictures taken in existing light do not require the presence of lighting equipment, they are often quite natural-looking. However, correct exposure is important to insure a good image.

dark as the scene. To reduce exposure, use either a faster shutter speed (1/125 second if 1/60 second is indicated) or a smaller aperture (*f*/8 if *f*/5.6 is indicated). On automatic SLR cameras, you can reduce exposure by setting the exposure compensation control to −1/2 or −1 stop.

Some SLR cameras and many non-SLR cameras have a built-in flash that fires automatically in dim light. If your camera has a built-in flash, check the manual (or take some test shots) to see if the flash fires automatically in dim light. If it does, the camera may have a control to turn off the flash. If there is none, try covering the flash before it fires. Review your camera manual for any tips on using your particular camera in existing light.

Autofocus SLR cameras will usually function well even in very dim light. But very uniform dim lighting may confuse some autofocus SLRs. If it does, simply switch the focus mode to manual and focus the lens by hand.

With print films, it's better to overexpose slightly than risk underexposure, so follow the camera meter's exposure settings. When you turn the film in for processing, you can write a note to inform the photofinisher that the prints should be dark because the scenes were dark. If your prints appear too light, it's because the printing equipment tries to lighten the photo to match a built-in program that says "normal" scenes have a certain brightness. In that case return the prints and ask that they be made darker.

Scenes with bright and dark areas. Scenes with uneven illumination are common in existing-light photography. Uneven lighting often makes your pictures more dramatic, but you will need to exercise more care in making exposure-meter readings under these conditions. Many existing-light scenes—downtown streets and outdoor holiday lighting at night, for example—include large dark areas and smaller lighted areas. In pictures of these scenes, it's usually desirable to have detail in the lighted areas, with the dark or black areas showing little or no detail. Expose for the bright areas and let the dark areas go black.

Joy Freis

**Scenes which have
both bright and
dark areas
challenge the
photographer by
making the proper
exposure critical.**

Brett Froomer

These photographs show how the lighting can affect your images. In the photograph at top, the girl is charmingly portrayed; in the lower photograph, the mood is more pensive with her face half in shadow.

USING EXISTING LIGHT

You'll find uneven lighting indoors as well. For example, at home, lamps and windows (during the day) can fool the meter. Spotlights illuminating performers in shows and nightclub acts also provide uneven lighting conditions.

A built-in camera meter is strongly influenced by large dark or light areas. As a result it indicates the wrong exposure when small, important areas are much lighter or darker than the large, unimportant areas. In these situations, move in to take close-up readings of the important areas. How you do this depends on your camera. With some older cameras you make the meter reading and then set the shutter speed and lens opening manually. Cameras that set exposure automatically may have a meter-hold button or a shutter release that will hold the meter reading when you depress the release partway. See your camera manual for specific instructions for your camera.

Some cameras even have special metering patterns (called matrix or evaluative metering) that can give correct exposure for scenes with bright lights and deep shadows. With such cameras, you may not need to take close-up meter readings (although it wouldn't hurt). Again, refer to your camera manual.

If different exposures are indicated by your meter for different areas of equal importance in the same scene, set the exposure halfway between the correct exposures for the lightest important area and the darkest important area. For example, if 1/30 second at f/5.6 is correct for the lightest important part of your picture and 1/30 second at f/2 is correct for the darkest important part, then 1/30 second between f/2.8 and f/4 is the best exposure for the picture.

Bright lights in the scene can mislead your camera meter, making the reading too high and causing underexposure. To get the correct exposure, make a close-up reading of your subject. When a light source, say a neon sign, is the subject, make a close-up reading of it and expose according to the meter.

For certain scenes that can mislead your meter or for situations in which it's impractical to make a close-up reading, an exposure table may be more reliable than an exposure meter.

PREPARING FOR EXISTING LIGHT

Daniel Barbier/Stockphotos, Inc.

In this photograph, the outdoors was intentionally overexposed to reveal the detail inside the puppet stage.

Spot meters. A spot meter is a reflected-light exposure meter that makes a reading of one small area in the scene at a time. (Some cameras have built-in meters that can make spot readings.) A spot meter is especially helpful when you can't make a close-up meter reading—photographing spotlighted performers at a circus, for example.

Spot meters are also useful when you use a telephoto lens. A telephoto lens includes only a small area of the overall scene that would be read by an ordinary, hand-held reflected-light meter. However, you should make more than one reading of different parts of the subject to determine the best exposure, even with uniformly lighted scenes. This is necessary because small areas of the subject usually differ in brightness. As a result, using a spot meter is more time-consuming and requires more experience than a conventional exposure meter.

USING EXISTING LIGHT

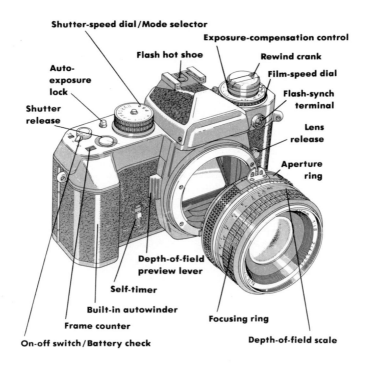

Shutter-speed dial/Mode selector

Exposure-compensation control

Flash hot shoe

Rewind crank

Auto-exposure lock

Film-speed dial

Shutter release

Flash-synch terminal

Lens release

Aperture ring

Depth-of-field preview lever

Self-timer

Built-in autowinder

Focusing ring

Frame counter

On-off switch/Battery check

Depth-of-field scale

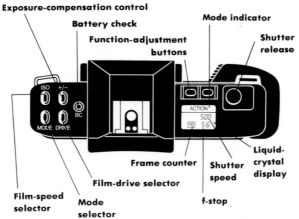

Exposure-compensation control

Battery check

Mode indicator

Function-adjustment buttons

Shutter release

Frame counter

Liquid-crystal display

Shutter speed

Film-drive selector

f-stop

Film-speed selector

Mode selector

The diagrams above include controls that can be used to adjust film-speed setting, aperture, and shutter speed.

Bracketing exposures. If you are doubtful about the correct exposure for an especially important photograph, bracket your exposures. Take one picture at the exposure indicated by your meter or suggested in an exposure table, and then take two more pictures—one at 1 stop less and one at 1 stop more than the estimated exposure. If you want even more insurance, make two more pictures—one at 2 stops under and another at 2 stops over the estimated exposure.

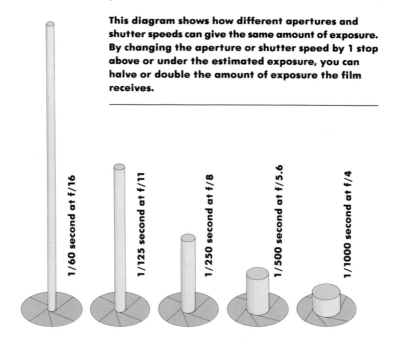

This diagram shows how different apertures and shutter speeds can give the same amount of exposure. By changing the aperture or shutter speed by 1 stop above or under the estimated exposure, you can halve or double the amount of exposure the film receives.

1/60 second at f/16

1/125 second at f/11

1/250 second at f/8

1/500 second at f/5.6

1/1000 second at f/4

TIME EXPOSURES

Although it's possible to take hand-held pictures of most subjects, you can take better pictures of certain subjects by making time exposures with your camera on a firm support. For example, time exposures of street scenes will record light patterns made by moving cars. When you make time exposures, you can use smaller lens openings to increase depth of field. Time

USING EXISTING LIGHT

Bracketing exposure in unusual lighting gives you a better chance of getting the image you want.

PREPARING FOR EXISTING LIGHT

exposures also let you take existing-light pictures with a slow lens or with a slower-speed film.

When you use long exposure times, the characteristics of your film can change.

This time exposure gives the impression of an empty escalator when, as evidenced by the shadowy figures at the top, nothing could be further from the truth.

The effects of long exposure times on color films. Most color films are designed for the typical short exposure times used in general picture-taking. At longer exposure times, approximately 1 second or longer for most films, film speed will begin to decrease and color rendition will shift away from normal.

USING EXISTING LIGHT

You can correct for this effect by using filters and increasing the exposure. It's not often practical in existing-light photography to use filters, but you can increase exposure to compensate for the decrease in film speed. You can avoid the problem simply by using shutter speeds shorter than 1 second, whenever practical.

Long time exposures are useful for some outdoor scenes at night, when color rendition usually is not critical, and often, neither is exposure. To compensate for the reduced film speed caused by long exposure times, increase your estimated exposure. For a 1-second exposure, use a lens opening 1/2 stop larger than indicated by the meter; for an exposure of 10 seconds or longer, use a lens opening 1 stop larger.

Al Satterwhite

The flowing water of this floodlighted fountain is beautifully captured in a long exposure.

Grant V. Faint

Long time exposures can create unusual effects such as the streaming car lights at left, or the unusual combination of fountain and fireworks below.

Grant V. Faint

USING EXISTING LIGHT

CHOOSING THE RIGHT FILM

The obvious choices in films are high- and very high-speed films. The answer is obvious because these films are more sensitive to light, so you can usually use a shutter speed of 1/30 second or faster—which means you don't need a tripod. Such films have high ISO numbers like 400, 1000, 1600, or even 3200.

Which of them should you use? For greatest versatility, use a color-print film with a speed of ISO 1000 or higher. Two such films are KODAK EKTAR 1000 and KODACOLOR GOLD 1600. With them, you can often use a zoom lens and fast shutter speeds, and still hand-hold the camera. The only drawback of these films is that they aren't well suited for photography in bright sunlight. If you expect to take photos in bright sunlight and in dim light on the same roll, use KODACOLOR GOLD 400 Film. Also use KODACOLOR GOLD 400 Film if you know you'll be taking pictures in fairly bright existing light, such as spotlighted stage shows. Films with lower ISO speeds give better quality than films with higher ISO numbers.

Daylight-balanced color negative films, such as KODACOLOR GOLD 1600 Film, give more natural colors in tungsten lighting than do daylight-balanced slide films.

Steve Kelly/Courtesy of Eastman Kodak Co.

When the light is fairly bright, as it is for some professional stage shows, or if you are using a tripod, you can use even lower-speed films, such as KODACOLOR GOLD 200 Film or KODAK EKTAR 125 Film. However, if the exposure is longer than 1 second, colors may shift unattractively (see "The effects of long exposure times on color films," page 21).

With any scene, many color-print films can be underexposed up to 1 1/2 stops or overexposed up to 3 stops and still give good results. Not so with slide films. Although some existing-light scenes shot on slide film will look good with a variety of exposures, many, such as spotlighted ice skaters, will require precise exposure. Daylight color-print films also give good re-sults under household lighting, such as tungsten or fluorescent lamps. Daylight slide films shot under tungsten light show a strong orangish color, and usually a greenish color when used in fluorescent lighting.

Bob Clemens/Courtesy of Eastman Kodak Co.

With push-processing, KODAK T-MAX 3200 Professional Film can photograph virtually any existing-light scene. Here it was rated at EI 3200.

USING EXISTING LIGHT

Steve Kelly/Courtesy of Eastman Kodak Co.

Very high-speed films (ISO 1000 or higher) can stop action in existing-light situations. In this photograph, KODACOLOR GOLD 1600 Film was used.

If you prefer color slides, try KODAK EKTACHROME 400 Film or KODAK EKTACHROME P800/1600 Professional Film. For black-and-white prints, use KODAK T-MAX 400 or KODAK T-MAX P3200 Professional Film.

There are three distinct sources of light in this scene: daylight streams in through the entrance, while green light on the floors above indicates fluorescent lighting; the warm, single points of light are tungsten.

Candlelight	Light Bulbs		Sunrise	Photolamp
1800 K	75 Watt	2820 K	Sunset	3400 K
	100 Watt	2900 K	3000-3100 K	
	200 Watt	2980 K		

USING EXISTING LIGHT

Color balance. The reason that photos from slide films taken under tungsten light (and to a lesser extent those from color-print films) appear orangish is that the light actually is orangish. And the light from many fluorescent tubes actually is greenish, which tints photos green. If you haven't noticed these tints, it's because the human visual system automatically adjusts slight color imbalances to be neutral.

Film, however, cannot adjust its color perception automatically. Color-balanced during manufacture, a film records the true colors given off by the light's temperature (see chart below). Since most people take pictures outdoors, nearly all amateur films are balanced for the neutral light provided by the sun. They are called daylight films. Electronic flash and carbon-arc spotlights produce neutral light. When daylight films are used with artificial light sources other than these, the colors of the photos are often not neutral, as just discussed. With high-speed color-print films, this usually isn't a problem since they are specially made to give acceptable colors with tungsten and fluorescent lights. Their colors can also be adjusted when prints are made.

The chart on page 28 lists filters you can attach to the camera lens to get more neutral colors when you use daylight film with

Daylight
5500 K
Electronic Flash
5500-6000 K

Overcast Sky
7000 K

Open Shade
12000-18000 K

artificial lights. The problem with filters is that they reduce the amount of light passing through the lens. When you're already in dim light, you don't want to further reduce it. As stated earlier, using color-print film will give good results in most lighting conditions.

Some professional films (and a few amateur slide films) are made to give good color with tungsten lights. They are tungsten-balanced. If you were to use such a film to take pictures out-doors in daylight, your pictures would be bluish. You could use a filter shown in the chart below to get neutral colors in pictures taken outdoors in daylight.

CONVERSION FILTERS FOR *KODAK* COLOR FILMS			
Light Source	KODACOLOR GOLD 100, 200, 400, and 1600 (Daylight) EKTAR 25, 125, and 1000 (Daylight) KODACHROME 25, 64, and 200 (Daylight) EKTACHROME 200 and 400† (Daylight) EKTACHROME P800/1600 Professional (Daylight)	KODACHROME 50 5070 (Type A)	EKTACHROME 160 (Tungsten)
Daylight	None	No. 85	No. 85B
Blue Flash	None	No. 85	No. 85B
Electronic Flash	None*	No. 85	No. 85B
Photolamps 3400 K	No. 80B	None	No. 81A
Tungsten 3200 K	No. 80A	No. 82A	None
Fluorescent	FLD	FLB	FLB

*Use a No. 81B filter if your pictures are consistently too blue.
†For critical use.

Tungsten illumination. Tungsten film is designed for use with 3200 K photolamps, but it's also excellent for existing tungsten light, such as the light from lamps with regular light bulbs in your home. Even though most tungsten lights are slightly warmer in color than 3200 K photolamps, we accept warm-looking pictures because most indoor scenes lighted by tung-sten illumination have a naturally warm appearance. If you use daylight film for tungsten light, your pictures will probably be acceptable, but they'll have a yellow-red cast.

These photographs show the difference that film selection can make. At the top, daylight-balanced film records the warm glow of the lights inside the house, while the outdoors is natural-looking. In the lower photograph, tungsten-balanced film renders the indoor scene natural, but creates an unusual blue cast outdoors.

Giuliano Colliva

In this case, daylight from a skylight offsets the green cast of the fluorescent lighting.

USING EXISTING LIGHT

Fluorescent illumination. Fluorescent illumination can cause odd color rendition in your pictures, since most fluorescent lamps are deficient in red. Daylight color film is best for fluorescent lighting, although your pictures will probably still look greenish. Tungsten film usually produces pictures that are much too blue.

You can improve the color quality of pictures taken under fluorescent illumination by bouncing light from an electronic flash off a white ceiling or by using an FLD (fluorescent daylight) filter over your camera lens. Because filters absorb light, they reduce the effective speed of the film. If optimum color rendition is important and the kind of lamp is known, you can further improve the color in your pictures by using the appropriate KODAK Color Compensating (CC) Filters. Selecting filters is sometimes difficult because there are many kinds of fluorescent lamps and each kind produces light of a slightly different color.

Generally you should use shutter speeds slower than 1/60 second with fluorescent lamps to avoid uneven exposure or underexposure because these lamps flicker in brightness. This flicker is caused by the alternating electric current and is not apparent to the eye, but it can be recorded on film with faster shutter speeds.

Mercury-vapor illumination. There are several different types and brands of mercury-vapor lamps in use today in many public places. Most are deficient in red light, so they often require heavy filtration for good color balance in pictures. Unfortunately, with some of these lamps, no amount of filtration will produce good color rendition.

Since it's improbable that you could find out the kind of lamps being used and some lamps require heavy filtration which would necessitate a large increase in exposure, it's impractical to recommend filters for mercury vapor illumination. Under this lighting, you'll get the best results on daylight color-slide film or KODACOLOR GOLD Film, but your pictures will usually have a blue-green cast.

Grafton Marshall Smith

Mark Romanelli

Mercury-vapor illumination can add compositional interest to your images, such the eerie-green streets of the photo at top, and the lamppost in the photo at the left.

USING EXISTING LIGHT

PUSH-PROCESSING

By extending the development during processing, you can seemingly increase the speed of many films (technically, you may not always be truly increasing the speed). This is called push-processing. It means that you can make a film act as if its speed were double or even triple its true speed. For instance, you could rate a 400-speed film at 800, or even 1600. Push-processing is most useful when you find yourself in dim lighting with too slow a film.

Most amateur color-print films aren't suitable for push-processing, while some professional color-print films, such as KODAK EKTAPRESS GOLD Films are. Best-suited, however, are KODAK EKTACHROME Films (slides) and KODAK T-MAX Professional Films (black-and-white).

Charles R. Shinaberry/Stockphotos, Inc.

You can use push-processing to boost film speed in dimly lighted situations and to freeze action. Here, in this night football game, it is put to both uses.

Patti McConville

If you want to use a film at a speed higher than its actual rating, it's usually best to double the speed. Set the speed on your camera, overriding the camera if it automatically sets the film's true speed. For instance, if you have EKTACHROME 400 Film in the camera, set the film speed at 800. Then shoot all your pictures for that roll at that speed. Find a photofinisher who push-processes film and indicate the speed you used.

If you have a choice between push-processing and using a higher-speed film with the same rating, choose that film. The results will usually be better. Push-processing reduces image quality: contrast and graininess increase, sharpness decreases. Details in shadows are reduced, and colors may shift. And push-processing costs more!

USING EXISTING LIGHT

TECHNIQUES FOR GETTING SHARP PICTURES

The slowest recommended shutter speed for picture-taking with a hand-held camera and a normal focal-length lens (50 mm) is 1/30 second. If you use a slower shutter speed, the photo is likely to be slightly blurred because of camera movement.

With a telephoto lens or a zoom lens adjusted for telephoto, you should use a higher shutter speed for hand-held pictures, or put your camera onto a tripod to eliminate camera motion. A telephoto lens magnifies the effect of camera movement to the same degree that it magnifies the image of the subject. When you use a 135 mm telephoto lens, the image is almost 3 times as large as that produced by a 50 mm lens at the same distance from the subject. Therefore, the minimum shutter speed for hand-holding a 35 mm camera with a 135 mm lens would be 3 times as fast as that used with a 50 mm lens, or about 1/125 second. When hand-holding a zoom lens, it's easy to forget to use higher shutter speeds when you switch to a telephoto setting. Some cameras will automatically increase the shutter speed when you change a zoom lens to a telephoto setting.

Focus carefully and use a high shutter speed to get sharp pictures.

George Obremski

PREPARING FOR EXISTING LIGHT

Taking long exposures of skylines requires steadiness.

Here are some techniques that will help you minimize or eliminate camera motion and obtain sharp pictures.

TO MINIMIZE CAMERA MOTION

- Brace yourself with your elbows against your body, and stand with your feet slightly apart for a good solid stance.
- If possible, brace your body against a solid object such as a lamp post or a wall.
- Hold your camera very steady and press the shutter release slowly and gently.
- Use a higher shutter speed, such as 1/125 second, when lighting conditions permit or when you don't need to use a small lens opening for great depth of field.
- For shutter speeds slower than 1/30 second, put your camera onto a tripod, table, or ledge; fasten it with a camera clamp; or brace it against a wall.
- Use a cable release or a self-timer to trip the camera shutter.
- Practice holding your unloaded camera as steady as possible and tripping the shutter.

USING EXISTING LIGHT

DEPTH OF FIELD

Depth of field is the distance between the nearest and farthest points in the scene that appear to be in sharp focus in your picture. Since depth of field is shallow with the large lens openings required for many existing-light pictures, it's important to focus your camera accurately or make sure that your auto-focus camera is focusing on the subject. Many lenses have depth-of-field scales which indicate the range of sharp focus. With some single-lens-reflex cameras you can also see what the depth of field will be when you press a depth-of-field button and look through the viewfinder. Check your camera instruction manual. If your lens doesn't show depth of field, your camera or lens instruction manual may include depth of field tables. If you want the greatest possible depth of field with a stationary subject, you may want to put your camera onto a steady support and use a longer exposure time and a smaller lens opening.

Luis Castañeda

Shallow depth of field can isolate your main subject and heighten the spatial contrast between foreground and background.

TAKING PICTURES
INDOORS

Is your approach to taking pictures indoors simply to mount a flash unit onto your camera and flood your subjects with artificial light? Did you know that, many times, a flash is not even necessary? If not, then learning how to take existing-light photographs indoors will certainly introduce you to a new way of looking at things.

Before you start taking pictures, it is necessary (as it is in many other situations) to ask yourself: What is the best way I can portray this scene? Often, the single-most important element in composition is the lighting. Lighting will affect the vibrance of color; and its presence or absence in parts of your scene will affect the overall exposure of your image.

Unlike direct flash, which may blot out detail in your subjects and can cast deep shadows behind them, using existing light keeps the scene as natural-looking as possible. With some attention to the direction and quality of the light source, you should be able to reproduce the scene to the degree that it greatly resembles what is perceived by the human eye.

Many of your best picture-taking opportunities occur in places where flash can be a nuisance. Flash may not be appropriate during a wedding ceremony in a church or during a stage show. Not only would it disturb the proceedings, it might not carry far enough to light your subject. At home, special occasions such as birthdays, anniversaries, and holidays, as well as such everyday events as the activities of a new baby, present excellent opportunities for existing-light pictures. Your subjects may not even notice you and your camera, so you'll be able to capture natural expressions.

In Part Two, we will discuss the various lighting situations encountered at home, such as daylight indoors and artificial lighting (tungsten), as well as lighting in such public places as museums and galleries, circuses and ice shows, houses of worship, in transportation, at school or sports events, stage shows, and hobby or trade shows. We will also discuss the best way to capture action situations, such as sports.

TAKING PICTURES INDOORS

HOME LIGHTING

Indoor scenes at home with existing daylight or artificial light are relatively dim compared with daylight outdoors (see color temperature chart, pages 26–27). Because the eye adapts to a large range of lighting conditions, you may not be aware of the low light levels in your home. At night, with all the lights turned on, the average living room with a light-colored ceiling has only about 1/800 as much light as you'll find outdoors in sunlight. Under these dim lighting conditions, a high-speed film such as KODAK EKTAR 1000 is a must for taking hand-held pictures.

Daylight indoors. You can take very pleasing pictures with daylight coming through the windows of your home—and you don't have to concern yourself with the weather. In fact, the lighting on overcast days is excellent for informal portraits indoors. It has a soft, diffuse quality which is flattering for

Joe Devenney

Using tungsten film indoors makes sunlight coming through the windows look blue and makes the tungsten light fixture appear neutral.

USING EXISTING LIGHT

Michael Salas

Brett Froomer

Daylight indoors often enters at an angle. In the top photo, sharp sidelighting heightens the drama of the subject. In the lower photo, the angle is less oblique and reveals much more.

TAKING PICTURES INDOORS

pictures of people. And it's even better when there is snow on the ground, since this acts as a reflector.

Existing daylight coming through the windows is usually brighter than the artificial light in a home. Opening all the drapes or curtains will raise the light level in the room—making it easier to get enough exposure—and make the lighting more even. You'll be able to record more detail in both bright areas and shadow areas.

On sunny days the areas in the room that are not in direct sunlight are usually best for picture-taking. But you can also get some good pictures when your subject is in direct sunlight near a window. Turn your subject's face toward the window, or select a camera angle that includes a minimum of shadow area. Bright sunlight lets you use higher shutter speeds and smaller lens openings, or even a slower-speed film than you normally use for existing-light pictures.

Gary Crallé

Daylight indoors can be a relatively bright, especially if there is more than one window near the subject.

USING EXISTING LIGHT

In high contrast situations, position your subject in the light, and use the shadows as a secondary frame.

David Garvey/Stockphotos, Inc.

A subject in front of a bright window may photograph as a silhouette. To avoid this, shoot from a position beside the window, or expose for the shadow side of the subject. If there are no other windows in the room to help lighten the shadows, try to stand so that the window is behind you.

Your camera meter can be misled by a bright window included in the scene. Either make a close-up meter reading of the subject or select a camera angle that doesn't include the window in the picture.

On clear days, when you're taking pictures in an area of the room that is not in direct sunlight, but where the blue sky is providing most of the light, try using a skylight filter No. 1A to reduce bluishness in your color slides. This filter does not require any increase in exposure.

TAKING PICTURES INDOORS

Artificial lighting. Artificial lighting at home usually includes brightly lighted areas around lamps and comparatively darker areas in the other parts of the room. Turning on all the lights in the room reduces the contrast and raises the light level so that you may have enough light to hand-hold your camera and obtain proper exposure.

A lighted lamp included in the scene may mislead your reflected light meter, so take a close-up reading of the principal subject, excluding the lamp.

House lamps with translucent shades are best for most existing-light pictures. Pole or gooseneck lamps, which give more directional light, are good to use when you want direct light on your subject or want a spotlight effect in the scene.

Turning on additional lamps will more evenly illuminate the subject.

Most household lamps have tungsten light bulbs. For color slides, use a color film designed for tungsten light, such as KODAK EKTACHROME 160 Film, to get pleasing color rendition in your pictures. In rooms illuminated by fluorescent light, use daylight color film without a filter. For color prints KODA-COLOR GOLD Films and KODAK EKTAR 1000 Film will give good results with both kinds of lighting without the use of filters. Since black-and-white film doesn't record the color of the light in the scene, you can use it with any kind of lighting.

LIGHT IN PUBLIC PLACES

Indoors you'll find exotic displays and dioramas in museums, lighted fountains in shopping malls, and beautiful flowers in bloom year-round in botanical gardens and conservatories. School plays, celebrating graduates, and leaping rebounders make up only a few of the other indoor opportunities.

Lawrence Berman/Stockphotos, Inc.

Many public places are lighted dramatically. High-speed films can save the day when you can't use a tripod or flash would lessen the effect.

TAKING PICTURES INDOORS

Using flash would defeat many photographs in which a glass case separates the subject from the photographer, and many museums do not permit the taking of flash photographs.

Museums and galleries. Museums, art galleries, and other public buildings provide many subjects for existing-light pictures. Some museums offer a variety of unusual sights, from giant models of prehistoric animals to priceless gems in exquisite settings. The lighting is often arranged to enhance the items on display. You can take advantage of this artful lighting when you take pictures by existing light.

The elaborate dioramas in many museums make especially good subjects for taking existing-light pictures. Since dioramas usually have painted backgrounds, use a large lens opening to throw the background slightly out of focus, thus making the scene appear more realistic.

Some museums and galleries don't allow picture-taking, although these restrictions aren't too common. Others do not permit the use of tripods or flash units but do permit you to hand-hold your camera for taking pictures by existing light. It's a good idea to check with the museum personnel before taking pictures. You may even want to telephone the museum ahead of time.

USING EXISTING LIGHT

Many museums, such as these, are well-lit by skylights and large windows. This lighting makes exposure less tricky, if not less critical.

Gary Cralle

Jake Rajs

TAKING PICTURES INDOORS

Circuses and ice shows. Photographing these colorful spectaculars by existing light is a natural because they are well-lighted and the subjects are usually too far away for you to use flash. The brilliant costumes and lighting give outstanding results with color film. Get a printed program for the show to help you plan your picture-taking.

The lighting at circuses and ice shows is provided by two general kinds of light—carbon-arc spotlights and general tungsten lighting. When shooting color-print film use KODACOLOR GOLD 1600 or KODAK EKTAR 1000 Film. With-slide film, you can use either daylight- or tungsten-balanced film, although daylight film will give the best color rendition for carbon-arc spotlights and tungsten film will give the best results for general, overall lighting. When colored filters are used over the lights, both types of film will give equally good results.

Jerry Yulsman

Events staged under carbon arc lights will look more natural when photographed with daylight-balanced film.

USING EXISTING LIGHT

While tungsten-balanced film would more truly capture the lighting of these events, the warm colors of the tiger and fire will show best with a daylight-balanced film.

Jerry Yulsman

Co Rentmeester

Houses of worship. Many important family events like weddings and baptisms take place in houses of worship, where flash may be inappropriate. However, you can record these meaningful events by existing light without causing any disturbance. Take pictures of a wedding ceremony from the balcony, where you can be unobtrusive and can steady your camera on the balcony railing. Take long shots that include much of the interior, then use a telephoto lens for close-up views.

Existing-light photography works especially well in houses of worship, where flash would either detract from the reflections of stained glass or interrupt proceedings.

Pamela J. Zilly

Joe Devenney

Giuliano Colliva

Many places of worship were built to admit large amounts of natural lighting, and thus are easy to photograph without using a flash.

Places of worship, often rich with historical significance or creations of modern architecture, make interesting and colorful subject matter for existing-light pictures. Their illumination may be primarily tungsten or daylight, depending on how much light the windows let in and the time of day. After you've taken an overall view of the interior, move in close for pictures showing the detail of the structure, such as intricate carvings and statues.

Stained-glass windows make unusual and extremely colorful subjects, too. Photograph them from inside with daylight shining through the glass. Move in close to the window to determine your exposure so that the meter reads only the light coming through the window. If you can't get close enough to make a close-up meter reading, try an exposure with the lens opening 3 stops larger than you would use for the outdoor lighting conditions. For example, if the sun is shining on the window, a typical exposure for a film with a speed of ISO 200 is 1/125 second at $f/8$. On a clear day when the sun isn't striking the window, try 1/60 second at $f/4$. It's a good idea to bracket your exposure.

Transportation. When traveling, take a few pictures of your family or friends inside the car, plane, or train to help build a story sequence for your travel pictures. Daylight coming through the windows provides the best lighting. Use an exposure meter to determine the right exposure.

Try to take your pictures when the ride is smooth, and hold your camera steady to avoid camera movement. Vibration can cause blurred pictures, so don't brace your arms or hands against any part of the vehicle.

It is said that "getting there is half the fun," but few people remember to record the journey!

USING EXISTING LIGHT

Patti McConville

Marcella Pedone

Train stations and other terminals are often buildings of historical or architectural interest.

School and sports events. Many school events like plays, parties, graduation ceremonies, and indoor sports contests make good subject matter for your pictures. In the daytime there is usually plenty of light for indoor picture-taking if the school has large windows. At night the light is dimmer, but the overhead lighting is usually sufficient for taking pictures.

Stage lighting in auditoriums is usually provided by tungsten lights. In classrooms, gymnasiums, and swimming pools, the overhead lighting may be tungsten, fluorescent, or mercury vapor. In the daytime, daylight is usually combined with the artificial overhead lighting. Find out in advance what lighting will be present and take along the appropriate film.

Daniel Teboul/Stockphotos, Inc.

A high shutter speed will freeze action while not distracting subjects with sudden bursts of flash.

USING EXISTING LIGHT

When photographing a game, try to get the players in action, as well as that "special player." And remember to check the type of illumination in the auditorium.

For sports events in a gym, determine exposure by taking a close-up meter reading of the gym floor area before the action begins. To stop the action, use the highest shutter speed that the lighting will allow. You can use higher shutter speeds with high-speed films like KODACOLOR GOLD 1600 Film, KODAK EKTACHROME 400 Film (Daylight), or KODAK T-MAX P3200 Professional Film. In addition to high shutter speeds, there are other techniques you can use to stop action.

Look for the peak of action. For example, when a basketball player is at the highest point of a jump, there is a split second of suspended action. Snapping the picture at the peak of the action freezes the motion in your picture.

The direction of motion has a large effect on stopping action with a camera. It's easier to stop the action if the subject is moving toward or away from you. You need higher shutter speeds to stop the motion of subjects crossing your field of vision at right angles than you need for other directions of motion.

Another way to help stop the action is to pan your camera with the moving subject. Move your camera smoothly to keep the subject centered in your viewfinder as you take the picture. Your subject will be sharp and the background blurred. This enhances the feeling of motion. Panning works best with a subject moving at a steady speed, such as an ice skater.

Subject distance is also an important factor in stopping action. The farther away you are from your subject, the easier it is to stop the action.

Stage shows. Musicals and plays provide beautiful settings for existing-light pictures. Stage productions are easy to photograph because you can use one basic camera setting for most of the show.

The camera setting for a typical professional stage show is 1/125 second at f/4 with KODACOLOR GOLD 400 Film. For color slides, film balanced for tungsten light will produce the most pleasing color rendition with stage lighting. Focus on a point in the center of the stage about 10 feet behind the foot-

USING EXISTING LIGHT

Existing-light photography allows you to take pictures without disturbing those around you.

lights to take pictures. You will have enough depth of field for most stages to make refocusing unnecessary.

If there's a lot of action on the stage, you can time your picture-taking to catch brief instants when the actors are relatively motionless. For example, most dance sequences include moments when the dancers pause as they finish a spin or change direction. Slight subject blur, caused by moving arms or legs, for example, can add a feeling of movement to the picture so that it does not look static.

If you use the basic exposure setting in the table on page 76, your pictures will become lighter or darker as the stage lighting changes, reflecting the mood of the different scenes. When spotlights emphasize one stage area, your pictures will capture the same effect. When all of the stage is dimly lighted, open your lens 1 stop from the basic exposure ($f/4$ if $f/5.6$ was indicated). If the lighting is very dim, open the lens 2 stops ($f/2.8$ if $f/5.6$ was indicated) from the basic exposure.

In stage productions, lighting is for effect. With a steady camera and a high shutter speed, you can use stage lighting to your advantage.

Don't worry if the lower part of your picture includes the heads of a few members of the audience. They will give the picture dimension and help frame the stage. For an unobstructed vantage point, try to get seats in the front row of the balcony. You may want to use a telephoto lens to get close-ups of the actors.

Remember that the people around you want to enjoy the performance, too. Be unobtrusive about your picture-taking so that you don't spoil your neighbors' enjoyment. Some professional theaters prohibit picture-taking during the performance because they feel it detracts from the show. One of the best times to photograph a stage presentation is during the dress rehearsal. You'll be able to get close to the cast and choose the best viewpoints for your pictures without disturbing an audience.

USING EXISTING LIGHT

Hobby and trade shows. When you attend an auto, boat, flower show, or some other interesting exhibit, you can get colorful and interesting pictures of the displays. The lighting for these shows is provided mainly by overhead lights, which may be tungsten, fluorescent, or mercury vapor. Individual displays often have their own lighting, which may be different from the general overhead lighting. Select color film for the light source that will be predominant in most of your pictures.

Hobby and trade shows take place in large spaces which are usually well lighted and offer many opportunities for picture-taking.

PART THREE

TAKING PICTURES
OUTDOORS

Lionel F. Brown

Once you start taking nighttime photographs using existing light, you'll be amazed at how much light there is and to what degree it can be exploited.

Existing-light photography is particularly appropriate for outdoor pictures at night, since flash would be useless in capturing twinkling lights at night, the beaming moon, fireworks displays, or streaks of lightning. While some of these subjects require more preparation, they may yield stunning results.

Be on the lookout for moving subjects that may make interesting time-exposures. One of the most common subjects for time exposures is traffic streaming red and white ribbons of light down the highway; the motion of some neon signs can also make a fascinating subject.

In almost every town or city, you will find possibilities for existing-light pictures. You can capture the colorful lights of holiday displays in your neighborhood, the myriad neon signs in a downtown street scene, and the fantasy atmosphere of fairs and carnivals.

When you go on a trip, there will be all kinds of opportunities for existing-light pictures. If you only take pictures outdoors in the daytime, you'll miss the chance to capture some of the most interesting sights of your tour.

Many places take on an entirely different look at night when the lights come on. Creative lighting plays an important role in enhancing architecture. You'll find that night scenes offer excellent pictorial possibilities, and night pictures add a change of pace to your travel pictures.

When you're sitting in the stands at a football game, the action is too far away for flash pictures. But existing-light photography allows you to make dramatic pictures of football and other sporting events outdoors at night.

In Part Three, we will describe various existing-light situations that occur outdoors, such as street scenes, outdoor holiday lighting, floodlighted buildings and monuments, outdoor sporting events, fairs and amusement parks, as well as fireworks and lightning.

Outdoor night scenes usually include large areas of darkness pierced by spots of light from signs, street lights, and buildings. The large dark areas in many night scenes make it difficult to meter a scene accurately. When you're photographing evenly illuminated subjects, such as floodlighted buildings, statues, and store windows, try to get close enough to take an exposure-meter reading. Take a small flashlight to help you make camera settings in the dark.

You can often get good results with a fairly wide range of exposures. Short exposures emphasize the bright areas by preserving the detail while the shadows go dark. Long exposures show more detail in the shadows and reduce detail in the brightest areas.

Outdoor fountains with lighted displays are most dramatic at night.

David J. Maenza

In many business districts, the lights never go out. This offers opportunities to make compositions emphasizing the buildings' geometric shapes delineated by light.

For outdoor picture-taking at night, choose either daylight- or tungsten-balanced film for color slides. Pictures taken on tungsten film may look more natural, while pictures taken on daylight film will have a warmer appearance, but both films produce pleasing results. For color prints, KODAK EKTAR 1000 and KODACOLOR GOLD 400 and 1600 Films produce superb night pictures.

To take photographs at night, follow these simple steps:

TO TAKE PHOTOGRAPHS AT NIGHT

- Use a flashlight so you can see to make your camera settings under dim lighting conditions.
- Outdoors in cold weather, put your camera under your coat between exposures to keep the shutter working properly.
- A good time to take outdoor night pictures is at twilight, before the sky becomes completely dark.
- For pictures of aerial fireworks displays, put your camera onto a firm support and hold the shutter open for several bursts.

Larry Dale Gordon

The regular pattern of these street lights is made more dramatic by the twilight sky.

An excellent time to take pictures of outdoor night subjects is at twilight, just before complete darkness. Your pictures will show a rich color in the sky instead of just black. Lights are usually turned on at dusk, before the sky becomes completely dark. While there is still some light in the sky, about 10 minutes after sunset, you can make pictures at 1/60 second at $f/4$ on KODACOLOR GOLD 400 Film.

Street scenes. Signs in theater, nightclub, or shopping districts make brightly colored subjects for your pictures. If your camera permits double exposures, you can make several exposures of different neon signs on the same frame of film. By placing the signs in different locations on the film, you can create an unusual montage. Make a mental note of the placement of the sign for each exposure so that you will create a pleasing design. Check the instruction manual for your camera to see whether you can use this technique.

USING EXISTING LIGHT

Neon lighted districts and displays can be great subjects. The instructions with some Kodak films for existing-light photography provide exposure information for subjects like these.

Gary Crallé

Hank deLespinasse

Store windows often have creative displays strengthened by dramatic lighting. Take a close-up meter reading through the window and try to select a camera angle that minimizes distracting reflections from the window.

The best time to take pictures in business districts is on shopping nights when the stores are open, because more buildings are lighted. An opportune time to take these pictures is during or just after a rain. The lights will produce a myriad of colorful reflections on the wet pavement, adding interest to otherwise black, empty areas of your pictures. For an intriguing abstrac-

George Obremski

Photographing holiday lights can be rewarding. In this photograph, the snow's reflective quality enhanced the dreamy mood.

tion, move close to a puddle so that the reflections become the main subject of your picture.

Holiday lights outdoors. Around the holiday season, many neighborhoods, downtown streets, and shopping centers blaze with color. Buildings with outdoor holiday lights make good subjects for color pictures. If there is snow on the ground, you can get interesting pictorial effects by including the reflections of the colored lights on the snow. On very cold nights, keep your camera tucked inside your coat until you're ready to take pictures. Cold weather may make some shutters sluggish.

In the city, the year round interplay of lighting and architecture provides an interesting backdrop for holiday displays.

George Obremski

Floodlighted buildings, fountains, and statues. Many buildings, fountains, and statues look rather ordinary in the daytime, but at night they are often beautifully lighted. Try framing such subjects with an object like a tree branch in the foreground. You can make interesting comparison pictures by shooting the same buildings or fountains during the day and again at night.

John Lewis Stage

Try positioning subjects in front of floodlighted fountains for interesting silhouettes.

USING EXISTING LIGHT

George Obremski

Brett Froomer

Look for unusual situations. In the photograph at top, the floodlighted building was further enhanced by the light of a "fire ceremony" beyond, while in the lower photograph, the composition is made dramatic by the reflections in the calm waters in the foreground.

Outdoor sports events at night. Night sports provide excellent subjects for existing-light pictures. Outdoor events may be illuminated with tungsten light, although many modern stadiums have mercury-vapor lamps, which have a blue-green appearance when compared with tungsten lamps. Even if you use daylight film with mercury-vapor lighting, your pictures will appear blue-green because the lights are deficient in red.

If possible, use a very high-speed film such as KODACOLOR GOLD 1600 Film so that you can use shutter speeds fast enough to stop some action. Don't worry if you can't freeze the action completely: Motion that's a bit blurred gives pictures a feeling of action.

Allan Seiden

Experiment! It is possible to use accessories in existing- light photography, as this photograph taken with a star filter demonstrates.

Alfred Gescheidt

Jake Rajs

Outdoor sports at night usually require photographing in existing light, as flash would be of no use at such long range.

Fairs and amusement parks. Fairs and amusement parks become a wonderland of colored lights at night. The festive outdoor lighting that you'll find in these places is superb for existing-light photographs. You can take hand-held pictures of lighted buildings, the midway, and the many colorful signs. Since lighting is such an important part of modern living, world's fairs and similar expositions display the latest lighting innovations. It's truly an exciting world for your camera.

Tim Bieber

This time exposure of an amusement ride captures the gaiety of the fairgrounds.

USING EXISTING LIGHT

Fireworks and lightning. Fireworks displays are easy and fun to photograph. You'll get the best pictures of aerial displays if you put your camera onto a tripod and capture several bursts in the same picture by making a time exposure. Focus your camera on infinity, and aim it in the direction of the display. Although exposure is not critical, use a color negative film to make it easier to get a good exposure. A larger lens opening (*f*/4) will make the lines in the burst thicker and lighter; a smaller lens opening (*f*/11) will make the lines thinner and darker. Set the lens opening on your camera according to the proper exposure (see the exposure chart on p. 76), and with the shutter set on (B), keep the shutter open for several bursts.

Fireworks highlight an already colorful picture.

Grant V. Faint

TAKING PICTURES OUTDOORS

Grafton Marshall Smith

Time exposures of fireworks are intricate displays of light and motion.

If you don't have a tripod for making time exposures, you can get successful results by hand-holding your camera and using an exposure of 1/60 second at *f*/4 on KODACOLOR GOLD 400 Film (Daylight). Take your pictures when the fireworks bursts are at their fullest.

You can add interest and a feeling of depth to your fireworks pictures by including lighted buildings, a city skyline, lights reflected in water, or silhouettes of objects in the foreground. If you have a telephoto lens for your camera, use it to take close-up pictures of fireworks displays.

Since fireworks displays on the ground last several seconds or longer and don't move across the scene, you can use shorter exposure times. For ground displays you don't need a tripod;

USING EXISTING LIGHT

Eric Meola

Fireworks displays over a city skyline make memorable photographs, but finding the right angle is important.

you can take pictures by hand-holding your camera and using a shutter speed of 1/30 second or higher.

Taking pictures of lightning is similar to photographing fireworks, except that you don't know exactly when or where it will strike. To capture the lightning in your pictures, put your camera onto a tripod and hold the shutter open for one or more flashes. Since you and your tripod would be likely targets for lightning, be very careful to avoid open spaces outdoors. Take your pictures from inside a building through an open window or from some other location (not under a tree) that offers protection.

Because you don't know when or where the lightning will streak across the sky, use a normal or wide-angle lens on your camera. This will increase your chances of having your camera

SUGGESTED EXPOSURES FOR EXISTING-LIGHT PICTURES

Picture Subjects	KODACHROME 64 (Daylight) EKTACHROME 100 HC (Daylight) KODACOLOR GOLD 100 EKTAR 125 T-MAX 100 Professional	EKTACHROME 200 (Daylight) EKTACHROME 160 (Tungsten) normal processing KODACOLOR 200 KODACOLOR GOLD 200 PLUS-X Pan	EKTACHROME 400 (Daylight) normal processing KODACOLOR GOLD 400 TRI-X Pan T-MAX 400 Professional	EKTAR 1000 EKTACHROME P800/1600 Professional (Daylight) at EI 800* EKTACHROME 400 (Daylight) with push processing	KODACOLOR GOLD 1600 T-MAX P3200 Professional
Home interiors at night— Areas with bright light	1/15 sec f/2	1/30 sec f/2	1/30 sec f/2.8	1/30 sec f/4	1/60 sec f/4
Areas with average light	1/4 sec f/2.8	1/15 sec f/2	1/30 sec f/2	1/30 sec f/2.8	1/30 sec f/4
Interiors with bright fluorescent light†	1/30 sec f/2.8	1/30 sec f/4	1/60 sec f/4	1/60 sec f/5.6	1/125 sec f/5.6
Indoor and outdoor Christmas lighting at night, Christmas trees	1 sec f/4	1 sec f/5.6	1/15 sec f/2	1/30 sec f/2	1/30 sec f/2.8
Ice shows, circuses, and stage shows— for spotlighted acts only	1/60 sec f/2.8	1/125 sec f/2.8	1/250 sec f/2.8	1/250 sec f/4	1/500 sec f/5.6
Basketball, hockey, bowling	1/30 sec f/2	1/60 sec f/2	1/125 sec f/2	1/125 sec f/2.8	1/250 sec f/2.8
Night football, baseball, racetracks, boxing ‡	1/30 sec f/2.8	1/60 sec f/2.8	1/125 sec f/2.8	1/250 sec f/2.8	1/500 sec f/2.8
Brightly lighted downtown street scenes	1/30 sec f/2	1/30 sec f/2.8	1/60 sec f/2.8	1/60 sec f/4	1/125 sec f/4
Brightly lighted nightclub or theatre districts	1/30 sec f/2.8	1/30 sec f/4	1/60 sec f/4	1/125 sec f/4	1/250 sec f/4
Store windows at night	1/30 sec f/2.8	1/30 sec f/4	1/60 sec f/4	1/60 sec f/5.6	1/125 sec f/5.6
Floodlighted buildings, fountains, monuments	1 sec f/4	1/2 sec f/4	1/15 sec f/2	1/30 sec f/2	1/30 sec f/2.8
Fairs, amusement parks at night	1/15 sec f/2	1/30 sec f/2	1/30 sec f/2.8	1/60 sec f/2.8	1/60 sec f/4
Skyline— 10 minutes after sunset	1/30 sec f/4	1/60 sec f/4	1/60 sec f/5.6	1/125 sec f/5.6	1/125 sec f/8
Burning buildings, bonfires, campfires	1/30 sec f/2.8	1/30 sec f/4	1/60 sec f/4	1/125 sec f/4	1/125 sec f/5.6
Aerial fireworks displays—Keep camera shutter open on BULB for several bursts.	f/8	f/11	f/16	f/22	f/22

*KODAK EKTACHROME P800/1600 Professional Film (Daylight) can be rated at EI 800 with 1-stop push-processing (Push 1), at EI 1600 with 2-stop push-processing arranged by your photo dealer, and sometimes even at EI 3200. To use the EI 1600 film speed, merely *decrease* suggested exposure in this column by one stop, at EI 3200 *decrease* exposure by *two* stops.

†Tungsten color film is not recommended for use with fluorescent light. Shutter speeds of 1/60 second or longer are recommended for uniform and adequate exposure with fluorescent lighting.

‡Shutter speeds 1/125 second or longer are recommended for uniform and adequate exposure with lighting from multi-vapor or mercury vapor high-intensity discharge lamps.

USING EXISTING LIGHT

Grant V. Faint

Photographs of lightning, such as this one, usually require extremely long exposures.

aimed in the right direction, because these lenses include more of the sky than a telephoto lens does. You may have to hold the shutter open for quite some time, so it's best to take pictures of lightning away from city lights and car lights. If there are no bright lights around, you can hold the shutter open for a minute or two when necessary, until the lightning streaks across the sky. If a car goes by, cover your camera lens temporarily with an object such as a hat so that the car lights don't spoil your picture.

CONCLUSION. Picture-taking is as simple or challenging as you want to make it. To make an outstanding photograph, it's often necessary to achieve the best balance of the many photographic principles involved. Under adverse conditions, it's sometimes desirable to compromise part of the picture-making process, such as exposure and development, to get the best possible picture under the circumstances.

GLOSSARY OF TERMS

Angle of view—The extent of the area seen by a lens. A wide-angle lens includes more of the scene than does a normal or telephoto lens.

Aperture—Lens opening. The opening in a lens system through which light passes. The size is either fixed or adjustable. Lens openings are expressed as *f*-numbers.

Autofocus—Used to describe cameras that focus automatically on the subject when you aim the camera so that the subject is within the autofocus marks or brackets in the viewfinder.

Backlighting—Light shining on the subject from the direction opposite the camera.

Bracketing—Making extra photographs at exposure settings to provide more and less exposure than the calculated or recommended setting—for example, at +1, +2, −1, and −2 stops from the calculated setting.

Built-in flash unit—A non-detachable unit that is a part of the camera. It is usually turned on by a button, but some units will automatically activate when the meter determines that the scene is too dark for proper exposure without flash.

Cable release—A thin cable that lets you trip the shutter without touching the camera; used to avoid camera movement at slow shutter speeds.

Carbon arc spotlights—Illumination that approximates that of electric flash.

Clamp pod—A camera support that attaches to a surface by means of a clamp.

Color compensating (CC) filter—A filter used to produce relatively small alterations in the color balance of a photograph to compensate for the color bias of a light source on the film itself.

Color-negative film—A film that is processed to form a negative image, from which positive color prints are made.

Color temperature—A measurement of the color quality of light sources; expressed in degrees Kelvin (K).

Color of light—See "**Color temperature.**"

Conversion filter—A filter used to balance film to a light source different from the source for which it is designed.

Daylight-balanced film—Film balanced to produce accurate color rendition in daylight or with electronic flash.

Depth of field—The distance between the nearest and farthest objects in a scene that

appear in acceptable focus in a photograph.

Depth-of-field preview button—A camera control that allows you to see the depth of field in the scene before you take the picture.

Diffusion—Softening of detail in a photograph by using a diffusion filter or other material that scatters light.

Diffusion filter—A type of filter that diffuses light. Diffusion filters come in varying strengths: No.1 is the weakest; mist and fog filters are considerably stronger.

Diopter—The reciprocal of lens focal length expressed in meters.

Direct lighting—Light that strikes the subject directly.

Existing light—Available light. In photography, existing light is the natural or artificial light that is already on the scene, including room lamps, fluorescent lamps, spot lights, neon lights, candles, daylight through windows, twilight, and moonlight.

Exposure—The amount of light that acts on a photographic material; a product of the intensity (controlled by the lens opening) and the duration (controlled by the shutter speed) of light striking the film.

Exposure meter—An instrument—either built into a camera or a separate, hand-held unit—that measures the intensity of light; used to determine the aperture and shutter speed for proper exposure. The same as a light meter.

Film speed—The sensitivity of a film to light, indicated by an ISO number or an exposure index (EI).

Film-speed setting—A camera setting—either manual or automatic—that tells the camera the speed of the film.

Filter—A piece of colored glass or other transparent material used over the lens to emphasize, eliminate, or change the color or density of the entire scene or certain elements in the scene.

Fisheye lens—An extreme wide-angle lens covering an angle of 180 degrees and creating distortion in the image. A full-frame fisheye fills the entire 35 mm format; a standard fisheye creates a greatly distorted circular image.

Fluorescent illumination—A type of illumination used in many public places; produces a greenish image, due to being deficient in the red spectrum.

***f*-number or *f*-stop**—A number used to indicate the size of the opening on most camera lenses. Common *f*-numbers are *f*/2, *f*/2.8,

USING EXISTING LIGHT

$f/4$, $f/5.6$, $f/8$, $f/11$, $f/16$, and $f/22$. The higher the f-number, the smaller the lens opening.

Focal length—The distance from the optical center of a lens to the film plane when the lens is focused at infinity.

Freezing action—A technique that makes an object in motion appear "stopped"; can be accomplished by using a high shutter speed or electronic flash.

Frontlighting—Light that strikes the subject from the front.

Graininess—The sandlike or granular appearance of a negative, print, or slide resulting from the clumping of silver grains during development of the film. Graininess becomes more pronounced with faster film, increased density in the negative, and degree of enlargement.

High contrast—A wide range of brightness from light to dark in the scene. Also describes the density range in a print, negative, or slide.

Highlights—The brightest areas of a subject and the corresponding areas in a negative, a print, or a slide.

ISO speed—A system of the International Organization for Standardization for measuring film speed.

Lens—One or more pieces of optical glass or similar material designed to collect and focus rays of light to form a sharp image on film.

Manual exposure control—A camera exposure system that allows the photographer to adjust aperture and shutter speed manually.

Mercury-vapor illumination—A type of illumination used in many public places; produces a greenish image.

Monopod—A one-legged camera support with a hinged head to which the camera is attached.

Normal lens—A lens that produces an image with perspective similar to that of the original scene. A normal lens "sees" the world roughly the same as our eyes do.

Overexposure—A situation in which too much light reaches the film, producing a dense negative or a light slide.

Panning—Moving the camera during exposure to follow a moving subject.

Point-and-shoot camera—An automatic non-SLR camera, usually with built-in flash.

Push-processing—Extending the development time of a film to increase its effective speed (using a higher ISO number for the exposure) in low-light situations.

Rangefinder—A focusing device on non-SLR cameras. The photographer aligns two images of the subject for proper focus.

Reflector—Any device used to reflect light onto a subject.

Reflected-light meter—An exposure meter used to measure the amount of light reflecting from a subject.

Reciprocity effect—The loss of effective film speed, change in contrast, or color shift that can occur when you use very long or short exposure times.

Selective focus—The technique of using a large lens opening to produce a shallow depth of field to isolate a subject in sharp focus from a blurred background or foreground.

Self-timer—A device that will release the shutter at the time for which it is set; used to avoid camera movement or to allow the photographer to be in the scene.

Shutter speed—The length of time that the camera shutter is open to expose the film.

Sidelighting—Light striking the subject from the side relative to the position of the camera.

Single-lens-reflex (SLR) camera—A camera that uses a prism and mirror to provide viewing through the picture-taking lens.

Spot meters—A type of reflected-light meter that makes a reading of one small area of a scene.

Stop(s)—Exposure increments. Each single-increment change in shutter speed or aperture represents one stop, and halves or doubles the amount of light striking the film. (Also see "*f-stop.*")

Telephoto lens—A lens that creates a larger image of the subject than a normal lens at the same camera-to-subject distance.

Through-the-lens meter (TTL)—A built-in camera meter that determines exposure for the scene by reading the light that passes through the lens.

Time exposure—A comparatively long exposure with a duration of seconds, minutes, or even hours.

Tripod—A three-legged camera support with a rotating hinged head to which the camera is attached.

Tungsten-balanced film—Film that has been balanced to produce accurate color rendition under tungsten light.

Tungsten illumination—Light from normal household lamps and ceiling fixtures (not fluorescent).

Underexposure—A condition in which too little light reaches the film, producing a thin negative or a dark slide.

Vignetting—Darkening or lightening around the edges of an image produced by masking during printing or using a filter with a smaller diameter than that of the lens.

Wide-angle lens—A lens that covers a wider field of view than a normal lens at the same subject distance.

Zoom lens—A variable-focal-length lens that can be used in place of a number of individual fixed-focal-length lenses.

GLOSSARY

INDEX

Aperture, 9; adjustment controls, **17;** for fireworks photography, 73; maximum, 9, 10, **10;** for sharp pictures, 35, **35,** 36

Bracketing, 18, **19,** 51

Camera, single-lens-reflex, 9, 12

Carbon-arc lighting, 27, 48, **48**

Daylight, as lighting source, **26,** 40–43, **40, 41, 42**

Depth of field, 18, 37, **37,** 57

Existing light: definition, 7; indoor, 38–59 (daylight, **26,** 40–43, **40, 41, 42;** in home, 40–45, **40, 41, 42, 43, 44;** in public places, 45–59, **45–55, 57**); outdoor, 56, 60–77 (at night, 62–77, **62–75, 77**); uneven, 12, 15

Exposure, 11–32, 76; bracketing of, 18, **19,** 51; for dimly lighted scenes, 11–12; for outdoor photography, 73, 74, 76; shutter speeds for, 12; for stage shows, 56, 57; time (*see* Time exposure); for unevenly illuminated scenes, 12–15, **13, 14**

Film: black-and-white, 25, 45; for carbon-arc lighting, 48; color balance of, 27–28, **29;** color-negative, 24, 28; color-print, 24, 28; color-slide, 11–12, 25, 45, 56, 63; daylight-balanced, **23,** 27, 31, 48, **49,** 63; for fluorescent lighting, 45; high-speed, 23, **25,** 27, 40, **45,** 56, 70; long exposure time effects, 20–25; low-speed, 24; negative, 12; for night photography, 63; push-processing of, **24,** 33–34, **33, 34;** for sports photography, 56, 70; tungsten-balanced, 28, **29,** 31, 48, **49,** 56, 63; for zoom lens, 10

Film-speed setting controls, **17**

Filters: colored, 48; conversion, 27–28; fluorescent daylight, 31; skylight, 43; star, **70**

Fireworks, photographing of, 9, 63, 73–75, **73, 74, 75**

Floodlighting, 68, **68–69**

Fluorescent lighting, 24, **26,** 27, **30,** 31, 45, 54, 59

Holiday lights, **66,** 67

Lamplight, 40, 44, **44,** 45

Lens: depth-of-field scale, 37; 50 mm, 9; telephoto, 16, 35, 50, 74, 77; for time exposures, 18, 20; wide-angle, 75, 77; zoom, 10, 23, 35

Lightning, photographing of, 9, 75–77

Mercury-vapor lighting, 31, **32,** 54, 59, 70

Meter, exposure, 11, 15; built-in, 15, 16; for night photography, 62; spot, 9, 16; for

travel photography, 52; window light and, 43

Movement, photographing of, 56, 57, 70; *see also* Sports photography

Neon lights, 64, **65**

Night photography, 62–77, **62, 63, 64, 65**

Overcast conditions, 40

Overexposure, 12, **16,** 24

Panning, 56

Portrait photography, **14,** 40, 42, **42,** 43, **43**

Public places, lighting in, 45–59, **45;** amusement parks and fairs, 72, **72:** art galleries, 46; circuses and ice shows, 48–49, **48, 49;** hobby and trade shows, 59, **59;** houses of worship, 39, 50–51, **50, 51;** museums, 46–47, **46, 47;** school and sports events, 54–56, **54, 55,** 61, 70, **70, 71;** stage shows, 23, 24, 54, 56–58, **57, 58;** transportation, 52–53, **52, 53**

Push-processing, **24,** 33–34, **33, 34**

Reflections, 67

Shadows, **14,** 39, 43, **43**

Sharp pictures, techniques for, 35–36, **35**

Shutter speed, 9; adjustment controls, **17;** for fireworks, 73, 75; for fluorescent lighting, 31; for reduced exposure, 12; slowest, 35; for sports, 56; for stage shows, 56, 57, **58;** for stained-glass window photography, 51; for sunlight, 42; tripod use and, 10

Sidelighting, **41**

Silhouette effect, 43, **68**

Sports photography, 54–56, **54, 55,** 61, 70, **70, 71**

Spotlights, 15

Time exposure, 18–22, **20,** 73; film for, 20, **24, 25, 29;** lens for, 20; light sources for, **26,** 27, **30, 32;** long, 20–25, **21, 22, 24, 25, 36**

Traffic, photographing of, 9, **22**

Transportation, photography related to, 9, **22,** 52, **52, 53**

Travel photography, 52, **52, 53**

Tripod, 10, 36, 46, 73, 75

Tungsten lighting, **23,** 24, **26,** 27, **40,** 45, **49,** 51, 59, 70; film for, 28, **29,** 31, 48, **49,** 56, 63

Underexposure, 15, 24, 31

Please note: Entries which appear in bold refer to captions.

DEP. LEG. B-9.474-90